CW00498539

My Networking Journal

Ellie Bowden

"Hi Everyone, I'm Ellie and I run Decor For Doors, creating handmade door bows for all occasions throughout the year"

This is my well-rehearsed introduction that I've used at networking meetings and on social media posts since I began my second business in January 2021. I've built relationships with other small business owners all over the world through networking — but keeping track of everyone I meet became quite overwhelming and has caused me to miss crucial follow ups that could have been really beneficial to my business and theirs.

So I began making more extensive notes, which I added to after meetings as well. Each person I meet has their own page with details of how they can help me and I them, possible collaborations, where we met, their social media information and areas for more information (do they have children, what are their hobbies etc.) that will help me connect with them in a real and genuine manner.

I've found it helps so much, rather than just having a notebook with scribbles in — I can have it all set out in an easy to see way, and can add to that person's page each time we meet. Each page consists of a lined page on the left for notes and a sectioned page on the right — these are meant to be used together for each contact.

And now I've decided to share this with everyone else! So please use this networking journal to grow your business and build those relationships, it's the best way to get yourself seen.

Ellie x

MY NOTES

Networking Contact

Name:

Business Name:

What Do They Do?:

Where Are They?:

How Can I Help Them?

How Can They Help Me?

Can We Collaborate?

Useful Information.

Facebook -

Instagram -

LinkedIn -

Website -

Where We Met:

Date:

MY NOTES

Networking Contact

Name:

Business Name:

What Do They Do?:

Where Are They?:

How Can I Help Them?

How Can They Help Me?

Can We Collaborate?

Useful Information.

Facebook -

Instagram -

LinkedIn -

Website -

Where We Met:

Date:

MY NOTES

Networking Contact

Name:

Business Name:

What Do They Do?:

Where Are They?:

How Can I Help Them?

How Can They Help Me?

Can We Collaborate?

Useful Information.

Facebook -

Instagram -

LinkedIn -

Website -

Where We Met:

Date:

MY NOTES

Networking Contact

Name:

Business Name:

What Do They Do?:

Where Are They?:

How Can I Help Them?

How Can They Help Me?

Can We Collaborate?

Useful Information.

Facebook -

Instagram -

LinkedIn -

Website -

Where We Met:

Date:

MY NOTES

Networking Contact

Name:

Business Name:

What Do They Do?:

Where Are They?:

How Can I Help Them?

How Can They Help Me?

Can We Collaborate?

Useful Information.

Facebook -

Instagram -

LinkedIn -

Website -

Where We Met:

Date:

MY NOTES

Networking Contact

Name:

Business Name:

What Do They Do?:

Where Are They?:

How Can I Help Them?

How Can They Help Me?

Can We Collaborate?

Useful Information.

Facebook -

Instagram -

LinkedIn -

Website -

Where We Met:

Date:

MY NOTES

Networking Contact

Name:

Business Name:

What Do They Do?:

Where Are They?:

How Can I Help Them?

How Can They Help Me?

Can We Collaborate?

Useful Information.

Facebook -

Instagram -

LinkedIn -

Website -

Where We Met:

Date:

MY NOTES

Networking Contact

Name:

Business Name:

What Do They Do?:

Where Are They?:

How Can I Help Them?

How Can They Help Me?

Can We Collaborate?

Useful Information.

Facebook -

Instagram -

LinkedIn -

Website -

Where We Met:

Date:

MY NOTES

Networking Contact

Name:

Business Name:

What Do They Do?:

Where Are They?:

How Can I Help Them?

How Can They Help Me?

Can We Collaborate?

Useful Information.

Facebook -

Instagram -

LinkedIn -

Website -

Where We Met:

Date:

MY NOTES

Networking Contact

Name:

Business Name:

What Do They Do?:

Where Are They?:

How Can I Help Them?

How Can They Help Me?

Can We Collaborate?

Useful Information.

Facebook -

Instagram -

LinkedIn -

Website -

Where We Met:

Date:

MY NOTES

Networking Contact

Name:

Business Name:

What Do They Do?:

Where Are They?:

How Can I Help Them?

How Can They Help Me?

Can We Collaborate?

Useful Information.

Facebook -

Instagram -

LinkedIn -

Website -

Where We Met:

Date:

MY NOTES

Networking Contact

Name:

Business Name:

What Do They Do?:

Where Are They?:

How Can I Help Them?

How Can They Help Me?

Can We Collaborate?

Useful Information.

Facebook -

Instagram -

LinkedIn -

Website -

Where We Met:

Date:

MY NOTES

Networking Contact

Name:

Business Name:

What Do They Do?:

Where Are They?:

How Can I Help Them?

How Can They Help Me?

Can We Collaborate?

Useful Information.

Facebook -

Instagram -

LinkedIn -

Website -

Where We Met:

Date:

MY NOTES

Networking Contact

Name:

Business Name:

What Do They Do?:

Where Are They?:

How Can I Help Them?

How Can They Help Me?

Can We Collaborate?

Useful Information.

Facebook -

Instagram -

LinkedIn -

Website -

Where We Met:

Date:

MY NOTES

Networking Contact

Name:

Business Name:

What Do They Do?:

Where Are They?:

How Can I Help Them?

How Can They Help Me?

Can We Collaborate?

Useful Information.

Facebook -

Instagram -

LinkedIn -

Website -

Where We Met:

Date:

MY NOTES

Networking Contact

Name:

Business Name:

What Do They Do?:

Where Are They?:

How Can I Help Them?

How Can They Help Me?

Can We Collaborate?

Useful Information.

Facebook -

Instagram -

LinkedIn -

Website -

Where We Met:

Date:

MY NOTES

Networking Contact

Name:

Business Name:

What Do They Do?:

Where Are They?:

How Can I Help Them?

How Can They Help Me?

Can We Collaborate?

Useful Information.

Facebook -

Instagram -

LinkedIn -

Website -

Where We Met:

Date:

MY NOTES

Networking Contact

Name:

Business Name:

What Do They Do?:

Where Are They?:

How Can I Help Them?

How Can They Help Me?

Can We Collaborate?

Useful Information.

Facebook -

Instagram -

LinkedIn -

Website -

Where We Met:

Date:

MY NOTES

Networking Contact

Name:

Business Name:

What Do They Do?:

Where Are They?:

How Can I Help Them?

How Can They Help Me?

Can We Collaborate?

Useful Information.

Facebook -

Instagram -

LinkedIn -

Website -

Where We Met:

Date:

MY NOTES

Networking Contact

Name:

Business Name:

What Do They Do?:

Where Are They?:

How Can I Help Them?

How Can They Help Me?

Can We Collaborate?

Useful Information.

Facebook -

Instagram -

LinkedIn -

Website -

Where We Met:

Date:

MY NOTES

Networking Contact

Name:

Business Name:

What Do They Do?:

Where Are They?:

How Can I Help Them?

How Can They Help Me?

Can We Collaborate?

Useful Information.

Facebook -

Instagram -

LinkedIn -

Website -

Where We Met:

Date:

MY NOTES

Networking Contact

Name:

Business Name:

What Do They Do?:

Where Are They?:

How Can I Help Them?

How Can They Help Me?

Can We Collaborate?

Useful Information.

Facebook -

Instagram -

LinkedIn -

Where We Met:

Date:

Website -

MY NOTES

Networking Contact

Name:

Business Name:

What Do They Do?:

Where Are They?:

How Can I Help Them?

How Can They Help Me?

Can We Collaborate?

Useful Information.

Facebook -

Instagram -

LinkedIn -

Website -

Where We Met:

Date:

MY NOTES

Networking Contact

Name:

Business Name:

What Do They Do?:

Where Are They?:

How Can I Help Them?

How Can They Help Me?

Can We Collaborate?

Useful Information.

Facebook -

Instagram -

LinkedIn -

Website -

Where We Met:

Date:

MY NOTES

Networking Contact

Name:

Business Name:

What Do They Do?:

Where Are They?:

How Can I Help Them?

How Can They Help Me?

Can We Collaborate?

Useful Information.

Facebook -

Instagram -

Where We Met:

LinkedIn -

Date:

Website -

MY NOTES

Networking Contact

Name:

Business Name:

What Do They Do?:

Where Are They?:

How Can I Help Them?

How Can They Help Me?

Can We Collaborate?

Useful Information.

Facebook -

Instagram -

LinkedIn -

Website -

Where We Met:

Date:

MY NOTES

Networking Contact

Name:

Business Name:

What Do They Do?:

Where Are They?:

How Can I Help Them?

How Can They Help Me?

Can We Collaborate?

Useful Information.

Facebook -

Instagram -

LinkedIn -

Website -

Where We Met:

Date:

MY NOTES

Networking Contact

Name:

Business Name:

What Do They Do?:

Where Are They?:

How Can I Help Them?

How Can They Help Me?

Can We Collaborate?

Useful Information.

Facebook -

Instagram -

LinkedIn -

Website -

Where We Met:

Date:

MY NOTES

Networking Contact

Name:

Business Name:

What Do They Do?:

Where Are They?:

How Can I Help Them?

How Can They Help Me?

Can We Collaborate?

Useful Information.

Facebook -

Instagram -

LinkedIn -

Website -

Where We Met:

Date:

MY NOTES

Networking Contact

Name:

Business Name:

What Do They Do?:

Where Are They?:

How Can I Help Them?

How Can They Help Me?

Can We Collaborate?

Useful Information.

Facebook -

Instagram -

LinkedIn -

Website -

Where We Met:

Date:

MY NOTES

Networking Contact

Name:

Business Name:

What Do They Do?:

Where Are They?:

How Can I Help Them?

How Can They Help Me?

Can We Collaborate?

Useful Information.

Facebook -

Instagram -

LinkedIn -

Website -

Where We Met:

Date:

MY NOTES

Networking Contact

Name:

Business Name:

What Do They Do?:

Where Are They?:

How Can I Help Them?

How Can They Help Me?

Can We Collaborate?

Useful Information.

Facebook -

Instagram -

LinkedIn -

Website -

Where We Met:

Date:

MY NOTES

Networking Contact

Name:

Business Name:

What Do They Do?:

Where Are They?:

How Can I Help Them?

How Can They Help Me?

Can We Collaborate?

Useful Information.

Facebook -

Instagram -

LinkedIn -

Website -

Where We Met:

Date:

MY NOTES

Networking Contact

Name:

Business Name:

What Do They Do?:

Where Are They?:

How Can I Help Them?

How Can They Help Me?

Can We Collaborate?

Useful Information.

Facebook -

Instagram -

LinkedIn -

Website -

Where We Met:

Date:

MY NOTES

Networking Contact

Name:

Business Name:

What Do They Do?:

Where Are They?:

How Can I Help Them?

How Can They Help Me?

Can We Collaborate?

Useful Information.

Facebook -

Instagram -

LinkedIn -

Website -

Where We Met:

Date:

MY NOTES

Networking Contact

Name:

Business Name:

What Do They Do?:

Where Are They?:

How Can I Help Them?

How Can They Help Me?

Can We Collaborate?

Useful Information.

Facebook -

Instagram -

LinkedIn -

Website -

Where We Met:

Date:

MY NOTES

Networking Contact

Name:

Business Name:

What Do They Do?:

Where Are They?:

How Can I Help Them?

How Can They Help Me?

Can We Collaborate?

Useful Information.

Facebook -

Instagram -

LinkedIn -

Website -

Where We Met:

Date:

MY NOTES

Networking Contact

Name:

Business Name:

What Do They Do?:

Where Are They?:

How Can I Help Them?

How Can They Help Me?

Can We Collaborate?

Useful Information.

Facebook -

Instagram -

Where We Met:

LinkedIn -

Date:

Website -

MY NOTES

Networking Contact

Name:

Business Name:

What Do They Do?:

Where Are They?:

How Can I Help Them?

How Can They Help Me?

Can We Collaborate?

Useful Information.

Facebook -

Instagram -

LinkedIn -

Website -

Where We Met:

Date:

MY NOTES

Networking Contact

Name:

Business Name:

What Do They Do?:

Where Are They?:

How Can I Help Them?

How Can They Help Me?

Can We Collaborate?

Useful Information.

Facebook -

Instagram -

LinkedIn -

Website -

Where We Met:

Date:

MY NOTES

Networking Contact

Name:

Business Name:

What Do They Do?:

Where Are They?:

How Can I Help Them?

How Can They Help Me?

Can We Collaborate?

Useful Information.

Facebook -

Instagram -

LinkedIn -

Website -

Where We Met:

Date:

MY NOTES

Networking Contact

Name:

Business Name:

What Do They Do?:

Where Are They?:

How Can I Help Them?

How Can They Help Me?

Can We Collaborate?

Useful Information.

Facebook -

Instagram -

LinkedIn -

Website -

Where We Met:

Date:

MY NOTES

Networking Contact

Name:

Business Name:

What Do They Do?:

Where Are They?:

How Can I Help Them?

How Can They Help Me?

Can We Collaborate?

Useful Information.

Facebook -

Instagram -

LinkedIn -

Website -

Where We Met:

Date:

MY NOTES

Networking Contact

Name:

Business Name:

What Do They Do?:

Where Are They?:

How Can I Help Them?

How Can They Help Me?

Can We Collaborate?

Useful Information.

Facebook -

Instagram -

LinkedIn -

Website -

Where We Met:

Date:

MY NOTES

Networking Contact

Name:

Business Name:

What Do They Do?:

Where Are They?:

How Can I Help Them?

How Can They Help Me?

Can We Collaborate?

Useful Information.

Facebook -

Instagram -

LinkedIn -

Website -

Where We Met:

Date:

MY NOTES

Networking Contact

Name:

Business Name:

What Do They Do?:

Where Are They?:

How Can I Help Them?

How Can They Help Me?

Can We Collaborate?

Useful Information.

Facebook -

Instagram -

LinkedIn -

Website -

Where We Met:

Date:

MY NOTES

Networking Contact

Name:

Business Name:

What Do They Do?:

Where Are They?:

How Can I Help Them?

How Can They Help Me?

Can We Collaborate?

Useful Information.

Facebook -

Instagram -

LinkedIn -

Website -

Where We Met:

Date:

MY NOTES

Networking Contact

Name:

Business Name:

What Do They Do?:

Where Are They?:

How Can I Help Them?

How Can They Help Me?

Can We Collaborate?

Useful Information.

Facebook -

Instagram -

LinkedIn -

Website -

Where We Met:

Date:

Printed in Great Britain
by Amazon

79818142R00061